Dea

To ...

miracles!

I Tracy.

Miracle Mantras

"Let the words of my mouth, and the meditation of my heart, be acceptable in thy sight, O LORD, my strength, and my redeemer"

Psalm 19:14

MIRACLE MANTRAS

Jincy Kelly

Printed in the United States of America

First Printing, 2018

ISBN: 9781798767337

www.Jincykelly.com

Table of Contents

PREFACE

Miracle Mantras was written from the notes I scribbled on my heart along my journey of learning to yield to love, to trust, to hold on to faith even while faltering, learning to see more, learning to know more, and ultimately to behold and to become more.

The scribbled notes grew at an accelerated pace after I made the decision to say goodbye to the 9-5 lifestyle of corporate America, and set my sail on the unchartered waves as an entrepreneur and writer.

The journey, the climb up the unseen ladder, brought a truer freedom; the discovery of new stores of light and heat, and a heart ablaze with raw revelations from the highest heavens.

Miracle Mantras are the stars you can pluck from the chaotic, unruly, yet grand sky of life – rub them, tuck them in your pocket, hold them close. These mantras are there to touch, to ponder, to play with, until they blend and bleed into your pores. Your heart will begin to beam a new shine and your soul will start to sing a new song, a new mantra.

My intention in writing this book is that when there is a wrinkle in your day,

an opposition,

a hesitation,

a silent sigh,

a lingering question,

that the words from the pages of this book would rush to soothe a wrinkle or provide conviction for some next step.

Above all else, that you would be reminded that the Eternal Hand is always close to you, longing to hold yours; longing to be intimately acquainted with you: face-to-face, heart-to-heart.

I dedicate this book to the opening of the storehouses of thrilling joys nestled within your heart, your mind, and your wild free spirit.

LOVE SINGS A LOVE SONG OVER YOU

Love sang a love song over us when we were born. Love has hovered over us as a protective shadow all of our days.

Love cheers us on when we are at the acme of our achievements. Love comes looking for us when we are in the darkest pit.

Love sits next to us when we are feeling low.
Love listens.

Love hears all the discordant notes inside of us
And orchestrates a beautiful harmony from it all.

Love keeps hoping for us.
Love never stops believing in us.
Love never stops chasing us.

♥ Mantra

Loving God, let the eyes of my heart and my mind to be awakened to feel and know this love that has protected me and pursued me.

On days when the battle was intense and I thought I wouldn't be able to go on, somehow I came through to the other side. Your love has kept me and led me out of darkness.
Teach me to be intimately acquainted with this love.

THE IDEAL JOURNEY'S WITH US

Every person lives in two realms – the internal and the external.
There is the Ideal of each of us, somewhere above, past the deep fog.
Being achieved little by little, but never quite fully achieved.
It is the vision of the Ideal – of who we are, or meant to be, that quickens the pulse.

And kindles a wild spark in the spirit, for the real, the unattainable.
Above the ebb and flow of life, the Ideal journeys with us, untainted by hindrances.

It keeps alive the perennial hope that the best is yet a little further beyond.
Life would be poor and wretched without this vision of the Ideal, journeying with us.

The One who planted the unique vision of the Ideal within the deepest part of our being,
Possibly has a moving target; as we expand and grow, the target seems to move.

Because there are no borders in His belief in us,
No boundaries in His love for us,

No division in His heart, toward us.
All the radiant stars shine on us, and urge us on, to pursue the Ideal vision.

♥ Mantra

I fix my vision on the Ideal, the Greatest version of me.

I will allow this vision of my highest self to spark a fresh fire within me today.

And in the places I allowed myself to lower my own standards due to disappointments, I will hit the reset and recharge button.

Because my Creator believes in me, cheers me on, and empowers me with strength to pursue this Ideal version of me.

BORN TO BE CREATORS AND CHANGE MAKERS

Books, pages, words – worlds have been created by them.

Our Creator knew we would need books.

But He didn't create paper. He created Trees.

And built within the gaping parts of our inner beings,

The gift of imagination, wonder and ingenuity.

The thirst to create something valuable with our thoughts. Our hands.

To explore. To find solutions. To conquer.

To transform some small part of our world,

Into the clear mental images that roam around in the corners of our mind.

The exciting whispers that move through the aisles of our spirit.

We are happiest when we bring our touch of creativity into the routine rhythms of our day. ♥

♥ Mantra

I choose to see myself as a creator – to usher change and reshape things around me, especially the things that bother me the most, instead of just grumbling and griping about it.

It may be possible that the thing that brings me the most discontent may well be the holy grail I need to embark on, to explore and to find a solution.

My greatest pain will then become my greatest gain.

THE SPACIOUS PROVIDER

The Spacious Provider comes seeking the corners of our life we stitched together with threads of compromise.

Inspecting the dreams we put to sleep, in the roar of life's disappointments.

Gently, He undoes the stitches one by one that hold us in smaller streams.

Floods our life with the fire of new possibilities He places before us.

Invites us to stand in joyful waters of promise as they rise up to our ankles, our waist.

He shatters the shadows, bursts through, offering us more of life in every area.

He will never stop giving us Fullness of Life.

♥ Mantra

God help me to search the areas of my life in which I have settled and compromised. Help me to leave the smaller streams and stand in the ocean of Your promises and dare to believe for greater things.

OUR LITTLE LIVES MATTER GREATLY TO GOD

Stars spin their dance within Your hands,

Clouds glide in shapes and patterns that You design,

Winds chime and waves dance for You,

Birds and beasts and the sky sing their sacred songs to You.

Yet, You are ever longing to listen to our heart's whispers.

Galaxies at Your command,

At least one hundred billion galaxies in the observable universe that You hold together.

Mere insignificant specks with feet in this vast ever-expanding spectrum of wonder,

Yet, Your gaze is intently set upon our little lives; our thoughts, our dreams.

You are the Author of the Beginning and the End.

Yet, You delight to write our story; Your hand You place in our hand,

Embroidering a story together, to be remembered.

Light of the living; longing to penetrate our every shadow with wild sparks of joy.

♥ Mantra

I stand amazed in the presence of a measureless and unfathomable Creator of all creation. I realize how small and insignificant I truly am in the grand scheme of things.

Yet, I am amazed that the Creator longs to be involved in all the minute, intricate details of my life.

Since I am learning that You are never too busy to heed to my needs, I want to invite You in and discuss this struggle I am currently facing. Give me your wisdom and guidance.

MIRACLE MAKERS

To watch the gleam of light that flashes across our mind in our alone moments today.

To listen to the enlightening whispers that gently sweep over our souls.

To honor the sanctuary of our intuition.

To believe that what is true for us in our private heart.

To trust our own self today – every heart vibrates to that iron string.

♥ Mantra

Let me be attentive to the flashes of inspiration that come to me today.

Let me listen to the voice of my private heart and walk wholeheartedly in that direction.

THE TRUTH IS...

Truth is, if you were to look through the glass to see into your unborn years,

You would see piles of Goodness laid up on the side of your private roads.

You would see mounds of Mercy piled up on the other side of your life's road.

The warm blood of the living God circulates through all your future roads.

Truth is, for all the severe frictions on the wheel of life, there is oil reserved.

Truth is, for all the outskirts and far-off reflections that are yet to be, an echo of triumph rings.

Hinging on a golden word that leaps out from the painted pedantry, sweetly inviting us to its secure home – Faith.

Today, this goodness laid up for me, was by way of the mountains calling to me, before sunrise.

Took a detour from my gym and found myself garlanded by the glory of mountains by a hiking trail.

'Here I am waiting for you' spoke Creation.

The view from jaundiced eyes were cleansed,

To become alive with the beating of a new heart, new vistas, new energy.

♥ Mantra

I will trust that goodness is prepared for me, for all the days of my life that are ahead, for all the days before me that I cannot see.

Goodness has been laid up for me for the good days and the bad days.

Today I envision piles of goodness and piles of mercy heaped up on the road I will travel during the next 24 hours of the day.

A PLACE ALREADY PREPARED, THE WORK ALREADY FINISHED

Maybe there is a place prepared for you and me, resplendent with the reality of all our dreams.

A place joyously prepared by God with all the finer details, throbbing.

The work finished for us since the foundation of the world.

The glorious end is already written.

Then with great joy, the Dream Weaver begins to relay the beats of his unique dreams for us, into the breaths we breathe, from the refined air.

The quickening flash of a wild thought like a jolt that reverberates through our being.

A furnace of churning dreams, beneath the external silence,

Its fumes, penetrating us at certain silent hours.

He waits on us to step on the line where the wonder of the vision becomes the sand beneath our feet.

He waits on us to enlarge our spirits and our minds to embrace how high and how wide the trails of his dreams for us extend.

Moving only in shining rays transfigures the common eyes.

To see the Sun forever singing a covenant song over us.

The power of Faith propels even the feeble and the weary to the horizon of dazzling brilliance.

By uprooting doubt, the heartiest poison that grows in the human spirit.

♥ Mantra

I lean in to believe that I am the handiwork of God, masterfully created. I have been created by God to do good works by co-creating with Jesus and the Holy Spirit. So that I can engage in the works which God has already prepared in advance for me to do. (Ephesians 2:10)

THE POWER TO ALTER OUR COURSE

Every species of property is preyed on by its own enemies.

Iron by rust.

Flowers by birds and butterflies.

Timber by rot.

Cloth by moths.

Provisions by mould.

An orchard by insects.

The heart, with disappointment.

The mind, with fear.

The soul, with being lost.

Only humans possess power to halt the natural course of decay.

Only humans possess the power to hold the heart rusted with disappointments and scrub it with the soft cloth of hope.

Only humans possess the power to pull out the arrows of fears, injustice, judgments: fermenting thoughts that spread and inflict the entire body.

Only humans possess the most advanced powers of the mind to reshape and recreate our days and our destiny.

♥ Mantra

I choose to rejuvenate my thoughts, my mind, and my future.

I examine my thoughts: my fears, my anger, my judgments and I now embrace my power to change: from victim to an overcomer, from fear to faith, from disappointments of the heart to bright hopes - I plant these life-altering virtues inside me today, as seeds buried in the dirt of faith.

THE JOY OF SURRENDER

To surrender to our Higher Power the nerve center of our desires.
The mainsprings of all our conscious thoughts.
To surrender to our Higher Power the alleys of all our hopes and dreams...
The side streets down which we walk at night,
The wooded areas and the swamps.

The thoughts and feelings reserved for innermost communion.
The fires that burn on different altars of our lives.
To walk together by the edges still untold...
To be fused to faith and the fire it sparks.

♥ Mantra

I surrender my thoughts and struggles to God.
I will share all my secret thoughts, my private hopes, and my dark thoughts with You.
I will lay them on the altar of surrender.
Because surrender brings an end to strife, and kindles a sweet aroma in my spirit.

STORMS, HURRICANES AND TSUNAMIS

Nature is not always kind.

The sky can turn black quickly, unleash thunderstorms.

Proud structures can instantly be reduced to rubble.

You wonder why nature will wage an open war against its children.

Even minds that bubble in the sunshine of optimism are forced to question such violent disruptions.

Maybe the network of the forces of control, by which we have held our lives, at times, need to be ruptured.

When the lights go out, to yield control of our lives to the One who calms all storms.

In the midst of storms, all our storms, this still remains true:

Sometimes God calms the storms,

Sometimes, the storms still swirl ferociously, and He calms our fears.

All storms still, when our questioning heart travels, to be tucked safely into His heart.

♥ Mantra

In this storm I am facing, I am forced to remember that as much as I try to control my life, there are forces in operation that are beyond my control.

And when things get out of control, even after I have done my best, I will still choose to trust.

I will yield my messy situation to the One who can calm every storm within me today.

THE POWER OF THOUGHTS

Thoughts are like trains running through the tracks of our mind.
They never stop to rest or to refuel.
They are eternal creatures inside us that never die.

Our thoughts, our ideas, our realities are perfected from age to age.
The progressive path – from the discovery of fire to the lantern to the light bulb.
Our thoughts can lead us from the lower rungs to the higher and highest realms.
To be held in the wonder of intoxicating possibilities.

We are responsible to expand the maps of thoughts and possibilities.
And hand over our collective enlarged boundaries as an heirloom.
As a precious deposit and a sacred trust, which the succeeding generation inherits.
It is an awful privilege and an awful responsibility.

♥ Mantra

I will pay close attention to the thoughts that run through my mind frequently, the good thoughts and the bad thoughts.
I make a promise to myself that I will be deliberate to expand the good thoughts within me, as each good thought will take me higher and bring me greater joy.

And instead of being a victim to the negative thoughts inside me that were given free rein, I will be actively engaged to turn down the volume of the negative thoughts that come to rob my peace of mind and my inner peace.

Holy Spirit help me, teach me how to stifle negative thoughts that come to rob my joys from the many minutes of my day.

THE SPACE BETWEEN NOTES MAKES MUSIC

It is the space between notes that makes music possible.
The structured pause, the silent rest.
The empty places....
Where particles scatter without making sense.

It is in the rest between lifting weights that muscles grow.
The sleep with least worry that ignites most muscular growth.
It is the walk in a park when freighted with the weightiest worry,
When restless strife is put to rest,
That the mind is kissed with a solution of nectar.

It is when a little hand reaches into a Bigger Hand,
Locked with the glue of trust,
That miracles are summoned to meet us on the unknown road.

Amidst all the chaos, trust is the silent song of peace.

♥ Mantra

Today I will make the deliberate choice to rest worry free as it is in this place that I will find the solutions I am seeking.

I will give my worries over to the One who can carry them for me and lead me to the perfect solution. And I will let my heart and mind sing the silent song of trust.

HAPPINESS

Happiness is a potent agent of purification.

It seeks to purify our faith.

It seeks to purify our purpose.

It seeks to purify our path.

It purifies our love.

♥ Mantra

Today I look at the important aspects of my life – hold it by the light of happiness to see if I am living by honoring my truth:

Does my job bring me happiness?

Does my faith bring me happiness? Is the path I am walking on bringing me happiness? Does my relationship with my partner bring me true happiness?

I will embrace one aspect of my life today that is not aligned with my happiness and will work on it until it becomes a path that brings me happiness.

GRACE STANDS BY YOU TODAY

Grace stands by the highway of your life today, inviting you.

It slips through the crack of your walls, as a bright light.

It slices through the sagging stories and presents its core, alive in its freshness.

It is scandalous in its generosity.

It offers a fresh start.

It wipes away the stain of shame.

It removes the rust of regret.

It slides in on the harp of a new song.

Grace invites the whole attention of your soul.

To remind you that it is as faithful as the sun,

As sure as the seasons,

Steadfast. Sustaining. Strong. In Her fight for you.

And invites you to participate in Her dance of devotion to you.

♥ Mantra

I welcome the gift of Grace into my life today – especially in my areas of struggle with health, finances and relationships.

I will remember to invite fresh Grace into my life every day.

I let go of strife and invite Grace to become my full portion of strength in my weakness today.

THE GIFT OF SLEEP

Increasingly, we are finding the simple things of life eluding us.

In 2011, some 40 million prescriptions for sleeping pills were dispensed in the U.S.

By 2020 the industry will be within eyeshot of the $10 billion mark.

Sad silences and broken stories haunt the night spaces,
When we feel the twist of every knife as it slashes our peace,
And drains love from our body.

The earth tenses, with whirling worry.

Yet, in the clear, cloudless heights,
There is musical perfection, the Ideal journeying always with us.
Surprise, sadness, love, disappointments, all threads on the loom of time,
That He weaves together into something beautiful.
And garlands the trusting mind with sweet sleep.

♥ Mantra

I trust and hand over all my worries to the All Mighty. Because I know He desires to orchestrate all areas of my life. He is working on my behalf even in the night hours. In trusting, I will be given the gift of sweet sleep.

TO REMEMBER THE STORIES WE WERE BORN WITH

Long before the world snuffed out our wildest dreams,
Long before the words inflicted from this world made us shrivel
inside a shell,
Long before the cynicism of the world seeped into our reality
Long before the trials of this world beat us down,
There was within the cry of the newborn,
A world splendid and abundant, wild and unique.
A cry in the newborn filled with fight and grit and glory.

It is found in the recurring echo within that drips with delight.
It is found in the sparkling waves that keep beating upon our soul.

Some of us fight to stay above the defeating clamor of the world.
Some of us fight to remember the stories we were born with.
And trace back to the steps of the faded footprints.

♥ Mantra

I will fight to remember who I really am, and who I was meant to be,
before the world told me who I should be.
I will fight to pursue my true path, so that I can bless the earth with
my gifts that are as unique as my individual fingerprints.

OUR LIFELONG NOSTALGIA

Our lifelong nostalgia to be on the inside of some door we have kept knocking on,

The door on which we have been knocking all of our lives, to be fully found and to be fully loved,

To be held in an orbit of rays that the soul is spellbound by,

That lifelong murmur is finally heard,

When navel-gazing on our problems finally loses its tenacious grip over us,

When we move from under its narrow, depressing awning.

Lifted to the gold tarmac to pursue things infinitely greater than our little lives of what shall we eat, and what shall we wear.

Now face-to-face, with the Author of the freshest waterfall,

Invited to drink from an ever-refreshing fountain,

The streams, which even at the lower reaches, prove to be intoxicating.

♥ Mantra

I know that my deepest hunger can only be satisfied by the one who created me.

The world with all its attractions will still never be able to fully satisfy all my longings. So I will yield my spirit to the one who is able to make sense of all my deepest longings and desires and fulfill them.

I will stop navel-gazing and look up to the One who longs to satisfy my deepest hunger.

SCATTERED PIECES OF MAGIC AROUND YOU

In the trap of the routine day, lies scattered pieces of magic.

Tender threads of joy from music that wraps around our soul to carry us to the doorstep of wonder.

Imagination, that transports us to our house of dreams.

The gift of taste with an array of delights that dance on our taste palette,

Integrity, that keeps our spirit sweet with a heart song.

Our routine path illumined by a new light, a new thought, today.

Our spirit set free on an open road with the expansive blue sky above us.

Invisible angels that come upon our bidding, to light up the sullen spaces.

Joy is not stumbled upon, but achieved.

♥ Mantra

Today I will soul search for the little pieces of magic scattered all around my life in the common hours of the day. I will set my spirit free to soar: while driving, while walking, while watching a sunset. I will be eagerly expectant for a breakthrough, a miracle.

BORN FOR BEAUTY

Born to live with freedom flowing through our veins.
Born to ride on the wild wings of our intuition.
Born to take flight into the wild unknown.
A Faithful Hand, holding ours, all through the journey.

Born to be found by Love,
Born to let the breath of Love's hope,
Breathe into our dark depths,
Awaken our weary bones,
Till we know that we have been found by Love

♥ Mantra

God longs to bless my life with full freedom and the truest, deepest love. I will stay focused on this truth, these liberating gifts, already prepared for me, ready to unravel at the opportune time, instead of letting my mind wander off to thoughts of lack and doubts.

SEE THE WONDER BEFORE YOUR EYES

See how sea waves are shut up behind invisible doors.
Where proud waves have to come to a screeching halt.
See how He spreads the clouds,
Formless majestic beings suspended in the sky.
Who can count the clouds?

See how He scatters lightning,
Bathing the depths of the sea.
See how He governs the nations.
Yet, somehow, He longs for a friendship with you and me.

♥ Mantra

I want to know You my Creator, and the creator of all of creation.
Teach me how to get to know You, the way You long to be known
– as a friend, not a heartless, authoritative, rule-based God.

THOUGHTS THAT BRING US HAPPINESS

Happy is the heart that glides through the garden of thoughts and picks the rose not the thorns.

Happy is the heart that takes the bleeding memory and places it on the altar of restoration.

Happy is the heart that looks not just on the five loaves and two fishes but the twelve baskets of overflow.

Happy is the heart that seeks not to vindicate, but seeks vindication from the One who is Truth.

Happy is the heart that replaces judgmental thoughts with a silent song of praise,

Happy is the heart that takes a wilted desire and waters it with songs of hope.

♥ Mantra

I will focus on the good things in my life today, so that it activates the vibrations to bring me more good. I focus on blessing the people in my life today so that **it** activates high vibrations to invite more great people into my life.

FATHER OF THE FATHERLESS

Father of the fatherless,

Whose protective shadow has hovered over us on the scariest days of our life.

Even when we wondered where You were,

Even when we were convinced that You had forgotten us,

You were there in the sidelines.

You knew that we would have the strength to endure. You knew we would become stronger through the trial.

You made sure death wouldn't touch us.

Friend of the friendless,

Who has carried us to be seated on the gleaming orb of the earth.

To share your heart's secrets with us.

Protector of the sinner,

Who has run to our rescue, and has fed us on the fallen way with the finest of wine.

Who has been quick to forgive us, eager to shower us with love.

Provider of the poor,

Who has poured forth the riches of your wealth, onto our spaces of yielded trust.

Nudging us to peek into the inheritance You have prepared.

Builder of broken things,

Who takes our shattered houses of hope we tried to build,

Even as we lament in our pile of rubble you whisper, 'Let's build it back together.'

♥ Mantra

I invite You God as a father, as a friend, and as my provider.

I invite You to build all the broken parts of me, as I work alongside You, to work out my healing, together with You.

A LIFE OF MIRACLES

We all establish lines along which we propose to live our lives.
Then there is the miracle of the working paper.

Whenever there appears in human history, a personality whose story extends far, in all directions,
The question of his or her working paper comes under scrutiny.
We want to know what were the lines along which he or she decided to live their life,
And the lines that they had drawn.

What stirred them to become elemental forces for us?
They astonish us by the full amount of life they radiated.
How they beat the primal fears that beset us all and lived in the prodigious glare of their convictions and affinities.

They become the solvent power to reconcile us back,
To remember our own devotions, our high calling.

Should we find ourselves by way of habit,
Begin to park our actions and ways of living in the common lines of the everyday grind,
They remind us that we can make our own working paper bright and miraculous.

♥ Mantra

I want to make the working paper of my life miraculous. I don't want to live an ordinary life. Because I know I was made for the extraordinary.

I will demand more from myself.

I will become better today than I was yesterday, last week.

I will take this gift of life that I have been given and make the working paper of my life, a miracle.

WOMEN, HOW YOU MUST BE CELEBRATED

It's International Women's Day,

When the true essence of a woman is celebrated.

Women are powerful, yet we have given up so much of our power.

It was in us women, in our wombs, that the worlds were meant to originate.

Henry Ford attributes his great success to his wife with whom he formed his first mastermind.

So do all the most successful men of the world.

I think of all the women who keep looking to men for value and worth,

When in fact, our value comes from recognizing the great worth God has already placed upon us.

We are not more powerful or less powerful than men.

Men are gifted with the strength to hunt and protect.

Women are gifted with the strength to nurture and inspire.

I think of the women who have been told to only say nice things,

Or to be quiet. Because that's what nice girls do.

But we women have been gifted with great insight,

To speak truth in boardrooms and in coffee shops.

We as women can return to the path where paradise is not lost,

We can become small but powerful generators of all things true.

We are the answer.

♥ Mantra

I will rise up to my power as a woman, filled with creativity and life-giving power. I will remember that I am the one to birth creativity.

I will remember that I am not weaker or stronger than a man.

I do not have to compete or try to prove I am better or stronger. I only have to seek to rise up to my inherent power and my calling. As men observe women operating from this place of wholeness, they will begin to honor the true strength of a woman.

WHERE OUR PURPOSE IS FOUND

Purpose is an invaluable defense against despair and depression.

Purpose pursues us all, like a restless itch upon the soul.

The dim, nagging echo screaming for more.

But where can you find it?

If only it can be prescribed by the physician and purchased over the counter.

If purpose could be purchased, it would be one of the most valuable commodities.

The purity of its essence, is rare.

Its brilliance shines brightest in the darkest room.

Our purpose lies nestled in the sacred folds of our sleeping soul.

In the shade and shape of light that uniquely awakens us.

Our unique purpose is quickened in the cracks that have crushed us.

We have the privilege of being the dispenser of this medicine called Purpose,

As we pull ourselves out from the unconscious current of habit,

Dive into the divine depths that bubble and gently swirl within our innermost being.

Our purpose is our redemptive song that becomes the redemptive song and solution for the ache of thousands around us.

♥ Mantra

I will spend time by myself, to seek out my unique Purpose. It is not a mystery that is meant to elude me.

My unique purpose is found hidden in the depths of me.

It is the thing that excites, sparkles and shines on all my senses in a way that it doesn't excite or awaken others.

When I acknowledge my true purpose and I am intentionally walking in it on a daily basis, it becomes my shield from depression and confusion.

I choose to live my life filled with purpose and passion.

SCANDALOUS GRACE COMES TO US TODAY

Scandalous grace. This is the trysting place we are invited to.

It is the banqueting table with a feast prepared for our all our hunger.

It is the place by green pastures and fresh streams where every thirst is quenched.

It is the place with a banner of love to shield us from storms.

All our angels wait on us for instructions; to act upon our bidding.

All the great men and women who have gone before us, wait and watch.

If we will choose to rise high and embrace the full grace.

If the waters parted to make a way for Moses, it can part for us.

If the torment and trails Job faced only brought him a double portion of blessings, then that is ours for the asking.

If David a young shepherd boy, with no leadership skills but a pure heart of love for God, and exceptional skill, at the menial tasks set before him, rose to inspire and lead nations, then that possibility becomes available to us.

How thrilling is this place of scandalous grace,

Beauty, Truth and Goodness is created here;

An open invitation for every hand that reaches out.

♥ Mantra

It takes courage to accept scandalous grace.

It takes a bold step of faith to walk the corridors of shame and regret and keep walking to the door of Grace, waiting to be opened.

Grace to fully accept and receive all the gifts life wants to shower upon me.

I will choose to embrace more grace into my life today.

WHEN EVERYTHING GOES WRONG

It was one of those mornings,

I slept through the alarm.

Woke up tired.

The coffee didn't taste strong enough.

The cat ran out of the house and I had to spend ten minutes chasing him down.

My car ran over a curb. A tire blew.

Roadside assistance never seemed sweeter to the ear.

Client appointment cancelled.

Yet, I was safe.

I could still wait in my car and enjoy the view of the mountains.

I could still walk to the gym.

I could still plug my headphones into my ears and get lost in my workout.

The gift of the sounds of music was there to thrill me.

The gift of a workout to produce the joyful rush of serotonin in my system.

The gift of taste that surprised me as I tried a new shake.

The gift of smiles.

The gift of a mind to always choose.

♥ Mantra

Today I will be intentional to search for the hidden nuggets of blessings even in the trials and troubles that drain my energy.

I will be intentional about seeking and searching for the blessings, discovered only through trials.

I thank You for the gift of music, the gift of smiles, the gift to always choose the outcome of every situation in life I find myself in.

WHEN WILDFIRES RAGE

Reason doesn't hold the reins when wildfires rage furiously,

Nor does logic play fair when floods overwhelm city streets and submerge houses.

In the weather sentences of tomorrow, there will be more tumultuous lines,

Much more than we have witnessed, thus far.

Who can hold back the violent Hand of the Heavens?

Who can shut up floods behind double-doors, when it bursts forth from the womb?

Who can journey to the deep depths of the earth to extinguish the source of fires?

Yet, if we let our hearts be stilled in torrents, there is a forgotten music in the storm.

It summons us to the inward parts, to a place beyond reason; to enter the gate of Trust.

Such bloom and light and bliss begins to clothe every questioning thought, within this Narrow Gate. Awakening an inward treasure that begins to sing the song of trust – loud, and louder still.

♥ Mantra

I realize that as much as I try to take full control of my life and situations, there are things that are outside of my control.

I have no control over storms and hurricanes, even the ones that occur in my life.

Upheavals that don't make sense.

When questions remain unanswered.

It is then that I must learn to yield my questioning heart to the power of trust.

There will be things that happen in my life that I will not be able to make full sense of, but I will still choose to trust that it was allowed in my life to make it work together for my good.

POSSESSED BY PASSION

Passion, and passion in its profoundest, is not a thing demanding a partial stage to play its part.

It demands the full engagement of every ounce of our energy.

Energy you weren't even aware you possessed.

It demands a tenacious spirit, at times with nothing to hold on to, but feeble faith.

It is severely tried in the burning fires of adversity.

But it continues to point with the most determined aim at its desired end.

As all the dross is burnt.

The circumstances that provoke it, are found in the dirt and in the hidden glory.

Nothing can stop its hallelujahs.

♥ Mantra

Give me courage to step into the passions of my heart.

I will run my race with a freedom and joy that only comes from living out my passion and true purpose.

OUR PACT WITH LIFE

We, who refuse to surrender to smaller ways of living,

We, who now refuse to entangle ourselves in the web of the lust of the flesh and the pride of life, that shrink our full joys,

We who run with the untamed fire: raw, throbbing, life pulsating energy.

We, who fight with the sword of truth, to destroy the untrue paths that lurk within us.

We, who bask in the rain from the stars as we turn on the hose of our intuitions,

We, who are lovers of the Eternal flame, burning on the throne of our hearts.

We, who will not settle for the dribs of life from rusty faucets,

We, who go seeking fresh waters from high mountains.

We, who chase angels carrying delectable promises for us on fluttering wings

Find ourselves in the quickening gasps of irrepressible ecstasies.

We, who still lift our banner high,

Trampled upon and smeared with dirt.

Though faint at first, but beating a little louder every day.

♥ Mantra

I will not settle for smaller ways of living.

I will not settle for a mediocre and average life.

I will not loiter about the stagnating places of gossip and idle chatter.

I will move forward a few steps today, toward the very best that life has in store, to offer me.

DEPRESSION – THE RHYTHM OF OUR TIMES

These rustic water troughs, built to create a waterfall, ran out of water this morning.

The soft music of cascading water was replaced by a jarring sound.

As I filled them up with water, the music of cascading waters resumed.

I think of the inner rhythm of our times –

What was meant to be beautiful sounds of living waters from within have been stifled.

Jarring sounds of depression looms large –

Within us, or in someone dear to us.

Sad thoughts swim aimlessly, to no sure destination,

When in fact, sad thoughts were meant to swim toward the Eternal Lids that never close.

And in the presence of Love, the languishing symmetry of sad thoughts that shape our life, was meant to be shaken and reshaped to joyous notes.

The permanent scar over our existence, was meant to be washed with wonder and glory.

As our thoughts were swept to the Creator of Love.

To endless oceans. To bottomless seas.

All our sad thoughts were meant to swim to the Eternal Lids that never close.

♥ Mantra

Today, I bring all my sad thoughts to God.

The creator love,

The creator of joy.

In exchange, I ask God to fill me with thoughts that awaken joy.

Feelings that strip away the sadness.

I want a transfer and an overflow of joy and endless delights streaming from the heart of God into my heart.

HER LOVE STORY

It was cold between her fingertips,
But nail scarred hands slipped between hers.
She stood in the corner of life, scarred, victimized and afraid.
But He swept her up, in a wild dance, onto the field of freedom.

She only saw the post-it notes of condemnation, in all her inner rooms.
But He walked right in and rended those notes,
Placed new sticky notes on those dirty walls.
Wild words, from His whispers to her heart,
That even lovers don't dare to say.

She only knew loneliness, especially at nights.
But Love came and sat next to her.
Love quieted the jarring noise of loneliness.
Poured a fragrant oil over every strained chord.

She did things she shouldn't have done, broken glass and fire around her.
But His wings shielded her. Every single time.
In the place of judgement and repercussions, she only found Love waiting for her.

♥ Mantra

I want to know this Love that is selfless, true and full of passion for me.

I yield my spirit to this Unconditional Love. I invite this Love to come flood all my rooms of shame, regret and hopelessness.

TO STAND AMAZED

Who gives light to the sun?
Who commands the morning to awake?
And causes the dawn to know its place?
Who orders the sun to go down in an orchestra of colors,
Who commands the purples to play? The reds to dance?
The oranges to swirl the skies at sunset?

Who makes darkness its swaddling band?
Who has comprehended the way to the dwelling of light?
And darkness, where does it reside?
Who knows of the paths to its home?

Who has seen the storehouses of snow?
Or seen the treasury of hail stored up?
By what way is light diffused,
Or the east wind scattered over the earth?
Who has divided a channel for the overflowing water,
Or a path for the thunderbolt?

Who causes it to rain on a land where there is no one?
In the wilderness in which there is no man?
To satisfy the desolate wastelands?
Who causes to spring forth the growth of tender grass?

♥ Mantra

God, I am amazed at the work of your hands. I will stop navel-gazing at the problems of my life and look up at the grand design of provision that is weaved through the entire fabric of all created beings.

I will live my life being aware and always reminded that You provide for all of creation and that You have a provision of abundance for my life.

WHEN WE WANT TO GIVE UP HOPE

Just when we are ready to give up hope,
To give up the fight,
When the light goes out from our eyes,
When the stars leave their shine above us...

Just when the last heaving breath finds us wasted and worn out,
When friction from the wheel of life becomes severe,
When the flame of our zeal has been reduced to dust...

There awaits a world ready to be born.
A world that waits for us to grow into and water.
As we reverence the golden thread of promise coursing through our Own Spirit.

♥ Mantra

I remember today that although my struggles are many and some of it seems to be unbearable, I am standing on the edge of a new world ready to be born.

I will stand tall in faith and not give up the fight. I will persist. I will continue to fight. Until I have overcome.

THIS BEAUTIFUL PLACE WE ARE INVITED TO

I know a place that blooms with wild fragrant life,

The firefly and the red bird and the yellow flower all seem to glitter in their own colors.

The breeze sprinkles gold dust of wonder over your mind.

A force of joy, from some unseen fountain, drowns your senses.

There is only the voice of love, and songs of love in every heart, in every flower, in every animal.

Fear dissolves within its pearly gates.

Every shade of hatred, greed, jealousy and anger crumbles and melts within every heart.

No black vein of thought courses through any mind.

Not the slightest shadowed judgment or arrogance alights here.

Every secret thought forms diamonds on a string that lights up our inner being.

A burning ball of delight burns within every spirit.

A prism reflecting an array of life giving shades.

All the forces of paradise blossom here.

Shared with the ones eager to touch the Eternal Heart.

The Brightest Sun that forever wipes winter from the human heart.

♥ Mantra

I know I was born for more than what I see or have now. I know that the only way I can step into the heights of joys and delights is by searching and reaching for the Eternal Heart, in whom my heart can be fully alive. In whom I can be fully found, fully be who I was created to be.

HELD BY HANDS THAT PAINTS THE SKY

Do you remember the evenings you stood by an ocean to watch a bursting sunset?

Or an ordinary evening that suddenly turned to purple and orange flames above you?

In the vast expanse of Majesty all limits melted...

Small thoughts transmuted beyond boundaries and your spirit soared to the edge of a new vibrant destiny?

These moments, when Love shows up in bold letters and parks itself center stage with no commas, no periods, no shadows?

The conviction that you are loved, and made for beauty beyond what can be fully fathomed?

Beauty and love like gentle salve soothing over the sorest spots?

Every evening, with every magical sunset Love softly taps upon our hearts,

Inviting us, along our routine paths, to be illumined by the majestic and the magical, to delight us.

Longing for our minds and lives to be inflamed, beyond borders, beyond our set boundaries...

Into all the magical hues Love longs to decorate our lives with, every evening.

♥ Mantra

When I watch a sunset, I will remind myself that God desires to infuse my life with a touch of the majestic and magic every day.

I will allow my mind to dream and wonder and paint my life with colors of glory, that stretch beyond boundaries and limits, just like the sunset comes to remind me each day.

THE VISION SCRUBBED

When the 5 am alarm slips to 6 am...7 am...

When the routine workouts become sporadic,

When the sales target hasn't been met.

When we find ourselves scribbling in the shadows of our goals.

We remember that we are never alone in our pure ambitions,

The lights of the Universe are turned on upon our goals and dreams.

As we look beyond the window to the sky, the vision becomes clear.

Angels are holding the corners of the rainbow of our dreams, although barely visible through the clouds.

Imagination leaps over walls, failures and fears,

To the field full of vision...

Bombarded with twinkling missiles within,

The vision still held up for you by your angels,

They scrub and scour it

And the vision is set upon your mind again with new vitality.

♥ Mantra

When confusion crowds my thoughts about the future, I believe that You God have a perfect way, and a perfect plan for my life, already designed for me. I offer my confusion to You, please reveal the perfect path. I will walk my path fully engaged, as an active participant, creating it, and birthing it to reality.

JOY IN THE NIGHT HOURS

As the night calls to rest my head upon the pillow,
Let the night hours be hours of visitation.

Let wisdom find its way to all the wanting parts of me
Let hope fill up the wasted veins
Let all the needy parts of me be restored
Let the hurting parts be soothed with the balm of healing.

Let false tenets lose their grip over my mind.
Let the noble pen write upon my soul, a new story of redeeming strength.
Let me be birthed with an idea in my sleeping hours
That will stir hearts and release fresh life.

Let the morning awaken me with angels sitting on either side of me,
Bearing gifts for me, for my success for the day.
And give me the grace to reach out and accept them without hesitation.

♥ Mantra

I will go to bed excited about the new things You, Holy Spirit, desire to teach and deposit into my subconscious being during my sleep. I will go to bed with anticipation and excitement. And wake up with a heart renewed and stirred with excitement.

FAITH IN OUR VIRTUE

Faith in our own virtue –
And in the virtue of those we associate with,
Is essential to the building of strong foundations,
In our individual lives and in the society we are all called to build.

To trust in our own self and in the work of our hands,
To trust others, that they will offer us value through their service.
Whether they look different or speak a different language.

To smash these valuable creeds of society,
Threatens the whole fabric of commerce.

Hate litters the world with mangled cripples.
But love from every individual heart,
Becomes a lighthouse that protects the rest of the world
And floods the individual heart with the first peace of a newborn baby.

♥ Mantra

Let me be a lighthouse bringing light to those who need it.
Help me, Holy Spirit to always look at others through your eyes of love and grace.
Grace to see them how You see them, past their shortcomings; focused on their greatness.

MAKING JUDGMENTS ROBS OUR PEACE

We are all quick and prone to making judgments; I know I am.

Every negative judgment I make in silence and in secret,

Robs me from my idyllic state of inner joy.

Caught in weakness, I still do ask God to teach me to see people through His eyes.

And somehow, He honors and responds to that intention.

I think we owe it to our own hearts and to the world around us,

To make it beautiful with our energy and our lives.

Especially when contrary forces are actively at work.

Goodness alone is worthy of being enthroned in our hearts and in this great nation.

♥ Mantra

Let me realize that making negative judgments about people makes me small and robs me of my inner peace.

Let me realize that thinking well of people enlarges my own heart and increases my joy.

Today, I will focus on believing the best about people I interact with.

TO WALK AS A FREE SOUL

To walk as a free soul
In a world teeming with fear-filled slaves.
Each day, to stand a little more courageously in our own light...

Breathing in its fearless air...

To live in response to our heart's calling,
To inflate our breathing with the trusting faith of a little child....
Fused with the graces of imagination
Is to hear music everywhere, touching the chords of life.
It is to hear deathless symphonies in our souls at all hours.

♥ Mantra

I choose to walk in freedom and not in bondage. I choose to live from my heart's calling, not from fear.

And when my frailty makes me stumble and fear, I will place my feeble hand in the Hand that is always reaching out to hold mine.

So I can run again with the music of my heart's calling.

INVITED TO PICK UP THE LAMP

It is a fascinating reality that we are not required to earn a master's degree,

Or pass a tough qualifying exam;

There are no prerequisites,

To possess the greatest force, the greatest power in this world – Love.

We have all been invited to pick up the lamp –
And to the light the way to Love.

♥ Mantra

Let me always be reminded of the power of love and its vigorous strength living on the inside of me.

I choose to be the one who holds the lamp, to light the way to love.

THE HIDDEN THINGS

In the shadows,
In the hidden echoes from within....
In the ridges and the creases....
It is in these places – what we give permission
What we hold, scarred or sacred,
That truly defines who we are.
And brings us low
Or
Takes us higher than we could ever imagine.

♥ Mantra

I will examine what I have given permission to reside in the hidden parts of me that no one else can see.

I will take time to uncover the thoughts and feelings I give permission to reside in the innermost parts of me. I will remove the dark secrets and the wretched ways that still reside within me.

Because I want to live a life of true freedom and true inner joy.

THE JOY OF UNITY

Unity is like a cloak of star-studded diamonds
That shimmers through all our thoughts...
It stitches our lives together with irrepressible joy.

Division is like a dagger that pierces our peace
It bleeds with boiling blood...
Its restless feet sink into boggy grounds of breakdowns.

♥ Mantra

Let me be the force that ushers in unity wherever I go.
I remind myself that when I practice unity in thoughts and deeds, it
will fill me with irrepressible joys.

THE GREAT POWER THAT PURSUES US

Who has laid the foundations of the earth?
To what were the foundations of the earth fastened?
Who drafted its measurements?

Who has wisdom to count the clouds?
Who can tip over the water jars of the heavens?
When the dust becomes hard and the clods of earth stick together?

Who knows when the mountain goats give birth?
Who watches when the doe bears her fawn?
Who counts the months till they bear?
Who let the wild donkey go free?
Who gave it the wasteland as its home?

Who gives the horse its strength?
Or clothes its neck with a flowing mane?
Who makes it leap like a locust, striking terror with its proud snorting? It paws fiercely, rejoicing in its strength, and charges into the fray.

See how He watches over all the affairs of the animal kingdom. How much more will He not provide and protect you;

Created higher than any other species. Designed to commune and whisper into the ears of the Living God.

♥ Mantra

If God provides strength to the horse, counts the months till the mountain goat gives birth, provides wastelands for the donkeys; then how much more will my Eternal Refuge not protect and provide for me in every way?

YOUR UNIQUE GIFT

I think each one of us was birthed with a Gift:

A fervent, solemn passion conceived in our hearts before we were birthed to the physical plain.

Through the years, and especially in the slim days, it leans to you, draws you to its centre;

Still a spring, still a fountain.

It is a unique inner treasure we are all born with,

To keep us alive, fully alive, even if extraneous delights should be withheld.

But millions are in a silent revolt against their lot.

Yet, there is a real wide world, a varied field of sensations and excitements,

That await those who delve into its inner expanse.

It is a spot of living fire, still twisting in the breath.

Still speaking softly from the bowels of our being...

And in those long midnight hours when morning seems weeks away,

Our unique gift, our unique fire, was meant to keep watch with us.

♥ Mantra

How thrilling it is to know that before I was birthed onto the physical plain, that there was a plan laid out for me to fulfill.

And a special gift to carry out my unique plan was conceived into my heart as I was being skillfully weaved in my mother's womb.

I realize how precious this gift is, so I will not hide my gift, but I will place it high as a light, so that others can be given hope and provided light in their search for their unique gift and unique path.

THIS I KNOW

This I know, that we all desire to be seen and heard for who we truly are.

I know a Porn Star who said she loved being in the porn industry because she could truly be who she was,

She was seen and admired.

Possibly when her own parents found too many flaws in her.

I know a Preacher who loved being on stage preaching, because he felt seen and heard.

It fed the thirsty insecurities running amok within him.

Porn Star and Preacher – both bleeding with the same issues...

This I know, that no media acclaim or fame can truly satisfy every heart's longing to be seen and heard for who we truly are.

This I know, that the invisible lines that stretch between our spirit to the Eternal Spirit that holds all galaxies and skies, is the only place our deepest thirst and longing to be truly seen and heard, is fully realized.

Love more true than the sun, as sure as the seasons;

Certain in every hour. Every minute.

Joy as real as the air we breathe.

♥ Mantra

I have come to know that I was created for a Love that cannot be fully satisfied by people,

I know that I was created to be fully known, to be fully seen for who I truly am, and the one place this can truly be a reality is in my love relationship with God.

Here I am fully seen, fully loved, fully accepted, fully whole.

Let me always seek to find my fill in this sacred place instead of placing this burden on people who were not meant to fully satisfy this deep longing of my soul.

YOUR VISIONARY LIFE STILL EXISTS

When life wears a visionary face full of life, but we are stuck in regular grind.

When it seems like there were so many futile attempts, useless jobs, wasted years...

Underneath the mundane footsteps there is musical perfection being orchestrated.

The Perfect One, journeying always with us, the heaven without rent or seam.

Creating with our life, through surprise, sadness, love, lack, disappointments...

A perfect story with all the threads on the loom of our times.

The visionary life still exists,

As long as we keep walking, canopied with our dreams.

♥ Mantra

Today I will stay focused on the greater vision for my life even though it seems far, and a distant reality.

Today I will walk with the remembrance of the highest vision of my life.

I will take a few steps forward, toward the highest version of my life.

TRUTH IN US REGENERATES

That which is false is false, and there is an end of it.
It is without the regeneration of life.
But Truth glows with a preservative power.
It is handed down generation to generation,
Quickening the heart and awakening the soul,
A never-ending fresh stream.

I was listening to a powerful song about God's goodness
At the end, the couple shared that they wrote this song after their little boy was taken to heaven.
In the midst of everything that appeared contrary,
They sang a new song.
They sang their truth.
That God was still good to them, even when they couldn't understand.

Sometimes, Truth glows the most in the darkest night.

♥ Mantra

Holy Spirit, show me all the false ways that reside in my beliefs. I give You permission to invade and break them down, and give You full permission to replace them with the ways of Truth.
I reckon, that this will come through new thoughts that I will need to embrace and continually bask in, until it becomes my new belief.

TO BE STILL AND KNOW

In the dark waters, to be still and know that He is God.
On the mountain top, to look up and know He is God.

When the night is holding on,
To invite Light.

To let the slender sound of Love seep in.
To let it percolate over memories of abuse, abandonment, and shame.
The unanswered questions find safety under His wings.

The Potter has power to mold soft, yielded clay.
Soft clay in the hands of the Potter
Over the Potter's wheel,
To shape the grand design of an overcomer to be etched into the clay.
To allow the grand design of greatness to be implanted into the clay.

In this new design,
For every unanswered question – peace prevails in the patterns.
For every adversity – the lessons learned are inscribed into a new striking design.

♥ Mantra

Let me be soft moldable clay in your hands God.

You are the potter, I am the clay.

I yield my life upon the Potter's wheel, to be molded into the grandest design.

THE CLASSROOM OF TRUST

To learn to have childlike trust requires so much more work as an adult.

Often, it ushers us into a narrow tunnel.

Dark, with no end and no light in sight.

We have to enter it naked and alone.

Forced to strip away all the rags of falsehood and doubt.

To gain the diamond and emerald studded robe that will never wear out

Embossed with precious jewels for every event that we passed the test of trust.

But first, it will leave us cold and naked, shivering and hungry.

Yet, the journey takes us into who we truly are.

And who we can fully become.

♥ Mantra

God, give me the willingness, courage and grit to go through life's toughest lessons of faith so as to gain the cloak of trust.

Until my trust in You becomes the imperishable shield of my life.

THE GIFT OF A THOUGHT

To preserve a raw, radiant thought uncorrupted by fears,

Or realistic concessions.

To summon every resource, seen and unseen...

To clothe the idea till skin begins to grow.

To feed it with living hope.

To guard this sacred ground that bubbles with the contained but roaring sound of new births.

This is our invitation.

This is our grace.

This is our glory.

♥ Mantra

Thank you for the gift of my mind, to think thoughts into reality.

Let me not abuse my thought world with negativity.

Today, I will fill my mind with beautiful, life-giving thoughts.

CHESTER BENNINGTON'S DEATH

Chester Bennington of Linkin Park, succumbed to the demons inside his head,

Sending shock waves across the nation on July 20, 2017.

His song lyrics cried out to the demons before they finally got him:

"I'm dancing with my demons
I'm hanging off the edge
Storm clouds gather beneath me
Waves break above my head...

Been searching somewhere out there
For what's been missing right here
I've been searching somewhere out there
For what's been missing right here."

Chester Bennington succumbing to the demons inside his head reminds us,

That if we can somehow find strength to be exposed to Precious Grace

To jump into the tidal waves of Endless Love.

Love that thrills.

Love that never lets go.

Love that pours over pain.

Love that sweeps over and fills old landmines of deep desolation.

Love that fills the empty cases.

Love that injects purpose into the meaningless vein.

Love that longs to rip through the thieving lies of old shadows.

This Love, it is the only true antidote to every demon inside of us.

♥ Mantra

Help me God to see that chasing money and fame will not fully satisfy me, or remove my inner demons. Only Your Love can do that. So I invite Your pure, beautiful Love to flood me, to overcome the darkness inside me that seems to want to stay glued to me.

I know that the power of Your Love can set all my inner demons to flight.

THE MAP OF LIFE

There are no defined paths to the map of life.
It is an ever-expanding grand horizon of new realities,
To those whose ears are tuned to its highest frequencies.
With a heart tethered to expansive faith.

A moment of splendor here and there in an unknown total
Of a great promise yet to fully unfold.

♥ Mantra

My life is an ever-expanding horizon. I believe my secret desires will unfold as new realities, as I keep focused, and believe that I have already received them.

I desire to embrace the full, abundant life that God has planned and already prepared for me.

THE SCANDALOUS POSSIBILITIES WE HAVE TODAY

It used to be that in centuries past, mainly the youth dreamed.

A form of delightful, chemical madness that dissipated in the coming years.

But we are living in glorious times,

Where the young who were too young to dream and the old who were too old to dream, can dream.

The convict and the victim can dream.

The young girl and the woman can dream.

Barriers of prejudice have become smoke.

Technological advancements and our march forward in every realm,

Allows us to be injected with a Divine drunkenness.

To seize a radiantly-imagined future as a possible reality.

Invited not just to participate, but to create it.

Scandalous possibilities – is what the men of old say – peering into what we have today.

♥ Mantra

I am so thankful that I can dream the outrageous dream my counterparts from a century ago could never dare to dream.

So I will ardently pursue my dream, knowing I have all the resources available to overcome every obstacle.

HEAR THE WIND CALLING YOUR NAME

Hear the Wild Wind calling your name again,

It rests not on the second thought, it scoops us up on the first flush of faith.

How it comes to us and where it will take us, is not always ours to know.

Just to trust that we can run with the whisper of the Wild Wind.

Run like the river

Follow the stars

Fly like an eagle

Ride on the Wild Winds, past the angels of darkness.

It's the place we'll always be home.

Where the flames burn brightest.

Knowing it will sink our hills, fill the hollows, bridge our rivers.

Run with the Wild Wind, faith beating upon our eyes,

This call, this adventure, is the one true place we'll always be fully alive.

♥ Mantra

I will run with the wild adventures beating upon my heart. I will chase the high call of God over my life, for then joy and bliss will fill my days.

I realize that true, lasting joy comes from running my race, abandoned to faith, on the wild winds of the Holy Spirit.

A CLEAN HEART

A clean heart is given clear sight.
It is offered the first peace known when it was tender.

The child stringing beads in kindergarten – happy, absorbed,
Commanded by every sight and sound, delighted with every new thing.
A full fascination for the bug and the bird.
The free, curious mind learned things that are not in scripts.

The air is pure. There is no odor of judgments or jealousy.
Beliefs are rife with all the bright colors of the imagination.
The heart of the earth beats with the clean, full breathing heart.

To cultivate a clean heart is one of the most untended tasks,
We dress our body with the finest clothes but forget to dress the heart.
Malnourished, its needs are reduced to a muffled whimper.

Only the self can provide the heart with the nutrition it needs to thrive.
Only the self can peer into the shimmering treasures buried at the end of the heart's steep, curvy road.
Only the self can make sense of the tremors of purpose coursing through its veins.

♥ Mantra

I will clean the cobwebs that cover my heart from neglect, from heartbreaks and heartaches.

I will let my heart beat again without being fearful. I will listen to my heart again.

I will nourish it, and provide it with the rich foods it needs: vulnerability, trust, hope, joy, faith.

As I resurrect my heart back to life, I will be able to live life filled with inner joys.

THE UNTAINTED WORD

I love the power of the untainted word.

In a world bombarded with opinions of people and politicians on Twitter and Snapchat and Instagram and Facebook,

The sterling clean, untainted word in these crowded social spaces is becoming rare.

Yet the untainted word still stands in its full strength, though rejected and forgotten.

It never stops shining. Its sweetness has no ending.

From Billy Graham who proclaimed his convictions across stadiums and passed to another world on Feb 21, 2018

To the passionate young Parkview students in Florida speaking their convictions across our sound waves.

The impassioned voices of the young sound their truth.

Their truth cuts through hypocrisy demanding that gun regulations be instituted for their safety,

The safety of schools in America.

Bold. Impassioned. Raw. Real.

Untainted words awaken the heart.

It spreads a certain sweetness over our calloused minds.

It lights up the dull path.

It is the seed that germinates with power to shape regions, change laws.

Long before the world crowded our untainted words,

Swept them to the sidewalk in a pile of rubbish,

Glittering words of truth roamed inside of us.

The untainted words, they got pushed to the border,

Under our skin of reason.

Yet, it still lingers as a distant rumble, seeking to revive our soul.

♥ Mantra

I choose to honor the untainted words that live within me, regardless of other's opinions. I want to believe and speak words that are not tainted with falseness.

I choose to seek and be around people who live their untainted truths.

THERE COMES A DAY WHEN THE WAR IS OVER

There comes a day when the war is over
When we can lay our weapons down,
Watch the fumes fading...

The war was fierce. The battle bloody.
It required every ounce of your thoughts directed to victory.
It required giving little credence to what was before you.
It required speaking life to the dead all around you.
It required every step filled with forgiveness and a wild fervor to stay the course.
It required washing yourself clean from the debilitating words of the enemy.

Now you stand on the summit with steady feet,
Take in the new panoramic view
New sights and surprises greet you.
The air is refined.

A door within you is opened to reveal a shape of you once thought unattainable.
The war, it expanded your mind, made your spirit vigorous.
You were refined in the severity of the war.
You were redeemed even by the sting,
Battle scars notwithstanding.

You pick up sharper weapons for the next war, the next adventure.
Paradise was found under the shadow of fierce swords.

♥ Mantra

I will look at the battles I face today with new eyes. These battles were placed in my life to enlarge who I am and to realize how much more I am capable of.

When the battle is over, I will step on higher grounds, housing a new and greater level of joy that cannot be taken away from me.

THE PURPOSE OF LIFE

"I'm here on the earth because a condom didn't work," Cody responded to my question about his purpose. A sense of sadness in his admission.

Cody, a 20-something attractive guy, with a good job at Wells Fargo bank, admitted he's been battling depression but is a fighter.

The challenge to stay positive can be a raging battle, when the secret story of your heart is founded on the fact that your birth was an accident.

He never hears the song that sings:
"Before you were formed in your mother's womb, I knew you.
I formed your inward parts in secret.
I knit you skillfully in your mother's womb.
You have been fearfully and wonderfully made."

He never hears songs that light a fire in his bones,
He never sees the design of purpose pulsating in the far recesses within him...
He never hears a love song being sung over him...

♥ Mantra

I will remember that I was created with purpose. When I feel unloved, I will remember that a love song was sung over me when I was born. That a passionate love song from heaven continues to be sung over me:
"You made all the delicate, inner parts of my body

And knit me together in my mother's womb.

You watched me as I was being formed in utter seclusion,

As I was woven together in the dark of the womb.

You saw me before I was born.

Every day of my life was recorded in your book.

Every moment was laid out,

before a single day had passed.

How precious to me are your thoughts, O God!

How vast is the sum of them,

Were I to count them, they would outnumber the grains of sand."

Psalm 139

THE PATHS WE TAKE

May the paths I take this week, bring me to greater heights.
May the thoughts I think this week, bring me more wholeness.
May the inferior thoughts be arrested and quickly strangled.
To let creativity and joy fill the soundtrack of my mind.

Let the notes and strains of each thought weave a sweet melody.
Let the lilt of a tender branch by winds remind me to keep my spirit tender and free,
Let the waves that swish and the clouds that swirl remind me that my prayers are being carried through waves and winds to celestial shores.

Let every choice I make find me on a higher step of true fulfillment.
Let every dream I dream open a new page of possibility.
Let every fire I face, burn away a little more dross,
So as to be refined to more of my true essence.

♥ Mantra

I will stay acutely conscious of every thought that enters my mind and arrest all unpleasant thoughts so that my mind and heart can bask in the fragrance of a joy-filled heart during all the hours of my day.

SURROUNDED BY GLORY

A sky that never sags with age,

The moon that never wilts through all ages,

Never failing to show up in glory, night after night, decade after decade,

The stars that never lose luster in their twinkle, through everlasting days.

Seas and rivers that never run dry,

Decade after decade, century after century.

There is no end to fresh waters available to revive our spirit day after day, year after year.

There is no lack of new ideas to awaken the dull and the dim thoughts.

There is no dearth of fresh fountains to drink from to quench our inner longings.

Every fiery red-gold-purple sunset to remind us that beauty and glory long to be the canopy over our lives,

Wonder waits to touch the edges of our common workday,

Eager to take us a little further, beyond the common horizon,

To the place where surprise and wonder wait to mingle with our senses.

♥ Mantra

I will not let my thoughts linger in the languishing pools of yesterday, or in the mundane, mediocre tracks of life.

I will not let my heart be dulled, by providing it less than all the magic it longs for.

I will actively seek to venture out a little further over the horizon, to the place where I come more fully alive.

TO SEE THE UNSEEN

If your eyes were to look into the unseen
You would hear a song being sung over you.
Lyrics of a song written just with you in mind.
The harmony has three voices – the Father, Son and Holy Spirit.

Goodness hidden along all the rocky roads this week.
A burden bearer ready to carry your burden,
In exchange for His burden that is light.
A Counselor to guide you along the unsure, crooked paths.

In the center of a tough and tender universe,
The heart of the universe is still beating for you.
Its axis arched to embrace your secret longings.

♥ Mantra

I remind myself today that the Universe is working for me in ways that I cannot see or understand.

I remind myself today that even if I am disappointed in myself, that God isn't disappointment in me.

In fact, my creator is singing a love song over me at this very moment.

FOUNTAINS IN THE DESERT

I used to associate the desert with everything dry and lifeless.

The analogy of the desert to all the trials of life always seemed fitting.

Not anymore.

After living in the desert, my eyes have been delighted with rare beauty that can only be found in a desert.

The cactus, the succulents, in all shapes and hues of green,

Tender, full of water in their leaves, they arise.

From dry ground. In the blazing heat.

Like they know how to find water even when it is dry.

Like they understand some hidden utterances, and have shiner insides.

Like it doesn't matter what the environment is all around.

Like their strength is steady, certain, even in hostile surroundings.

I know now that fellowship with suffering in our desert season,

Is when something long sleeping in the blood is awoken.

A rising tide within, begins to sing with the rocks,

A song that can only be composed in the desert season of our life.

A song full of life.

A song that can never die.

♥ Mantra

In the desert season of my life when everything seems to be dry and lifeless, God help me understand this: certain flowers and plants can only grow in the dry desert grounds of my life.

Give me the grace to allow You to bring a unique type of beauty into my life, that can only be birthed in the dry season of life, and in the desert.

THE INVISIBLE POWER THAT PROTECTS OUR LIFE

See how He holds the water's of the earth in the hollow of his hand?

See how He fills lightning in His hands and commands it to strike its mark?

See how He scatters thunder across the sky, and bathes the depths of the sea?

See how He spreads the clouds and makes garments for clouds,

Dressed on some days in thick darkness,

Dressed other days in soft fluffy white puffs.

See how He pins the clouds to the sky with invisible glue?

Who can count the clouds?

See how He makes waves dance with the seashore

See how sea waves are shut up behind invisible doors, as it bursts forth from the womb of the earth

Where proud waves have to come to a screeching halt. Saying this far you can go and go no more?

Will He not then bring to an end, the terrors sent to torment us?

♥ Mantra

God give me eyes to see the amazing mysteries of creation. And the lessons they are here to teach me. If You place a boundary line for waves, You will place a hedge of protection around, declaring to all my trials, and torments – this far you can go, and no more.

You will keep guard over my life, and keep me from being defeated by the forces that rise to threaten my life.

THE SWEET AROMA OF TRUST

To be married to trust is one of life's greatest blessing.

Trust travels with us as our closest friend on the unknown road.

It fills the open bleeding gnash of fear.

It soothes the scorched places of the soul.

It softens the heart hardened by disappointments.

It goes searching for the memories drenched in sadness, and wrings out hope from it.

It sings softly over our sorrows, the new songs of hope.

Trust takes the dust collected memories,

And places a renewed covenant ring on our secret longings.

Trust traces its steps to the doors of all our sins,

Takes each sin and carves from it, a stepping stool, to take us higher.

Trust will take a walk with us, giving us the courage to revisit the memories we blocked off,

It will never let go of our hand, and whisper that the painful memories have now become the sturdiest threads in the tapestry of our lives.

Trust turns every tear into a hallelujah.

♥ Mantra

Holy Spirit I ask you to teach me to trust you.

I make it my priority today to pursue acquiring trust as a virtue to be developed to its full potential within me.

I do not want to live my life jaded by past events that made me weary of trusting You and others. I choose to trust you wholeheartedly.

THE WEAK AND THE WILTED

I love that the weak and the wilted is who He goes seeking,

I love that his faith is so large, so firm; for the broken and the hopeless.

I love that He sits in the dirt, exactly where we are.

Delighted with all that we are – just as we are, nothing to prove.

Nothing in our hands to offer.

I love that His hand grabs ours and slowly leads us out from the muck,

Like a child being pushed from the comfort of the mother's womb,

Hesitant, crying, resisting we scream, we would rather stay in the stagnant womb.

But He knows there's so much more to be dazzled by,

So He pushes us out, reaching into all our aimless places of fear.

New constellations now orbit our mind and feelings,

The stumbling stone begins to sparkle.

This glitter, this luminous luster now plays on the top of our every hill and valley.

♥ Mantra

I thank you God that you came for those who need a healer, a physician. I thank you that your faith in me and for my life is far greater than the faith I have in myself.

When my faith is weak and when I falter, I will lean on you and rest in your faith you have for my life.

A NEW POSSIBILITY THROUGH ME

When we were little, we were often visited with quizzical, dazzling, original thoughts.

Along the walkway of life, the flash of an exhilarating idea visited us.

Hunches – whispers from the highest heavens.

But soon we blended in to the world's codes.

We planted our feet firm in the gibbering swamp of mediocrity.

I think that we are being invited again and again,

By way of that bold untried thought, to create a new possibility.

I'm creating a fitness product for women addressing an issue that pretty much everyone says is not possible to get rid of.

But then I heard God asking, "Can you dare to challenge the accepted norm?"

I think that we are often provided a dormant idea within our inner knowing,

The capacity to see, connect and make what had not been seen or connected before.

Everything we desire, but don't see, is the result of fear or inertia or a historical lack of someone asking:

"Why not?"

Explore the wild thoughts and hunches that were breathed into your blood.

♥ Mantra

Today, I give permission to the wild thought that may visit me like a bright beam. I will ponder over the creative thoughts that alight upon my mind, in my moments of rest, thoughts that in the past, I have often chalked up to them being random-wishful-thoughts.

I realize now that these wild thoughts as they visited me carried within them, the generative power to create that thought as a reality in my life. But I didn't dare to believe.

But today and all my tomorrows, I will pay careful attention to the hunches that visit me, for they are whispers from the highest heavens, sent to awaken a new reality within me.

YOUR LIFE GIVER'S INVITATION

I want you to run on greener pastures.

I want you to dance on higher hills.

I want you to drink from sweeter waters.

Because this life was meant to be beautiful beyond your wildest dreams.

Leave the stagnant murky puddles where fears and doubts and jealousy and insecurities thrive.

Leap on the wings of angles.

Saddle up.

Let life take you on its high adventures.

Because the kingdom of God is at hand.

All the beautiful things you imagined in your wildest dreams,

Arrive accompanied with an innate potent power to create into existence.

It is at hand – your hands, and mind, working diligently to create it.

The promotion at work, that vacation, the one true love,

That product or service you are laboriously creating,

The dream you are tossing around in your mind,

The intoxicating kingdom of riches being offered into your hands as a promise,

It is yours; to work out its reality, even today.

♥ Mantra

I accept the invitation to embrace the fullness of life. I accept the invitation to reach for more in my finances, health, love, career and family.

I choose to go after all the beautiful things promised and planned for my life.

These plans have in a sense, already been completed in the heavenly realm, they are completed in another dimension, and I need to simply align my vibrations and beliefs to the as-it-is-in-heaven state, in order to usher them here to the physical plain.

EVERLASTING LOVE

We all long for everlasting love. Because it is what has been prepared for us.
For us who accept this Eternal Love,
We will return to perfect, forever love, at the end of life's tunnel.
We all desire to be disease free and healthy, because this is our portion, already allotted to us.
We all seek an abundance of prosperity because this is the inheritance already assigned to our name.

The fighters, the seers, the restless ones, will relentlessly seek to bring these realities into the here and now.
We all have the power to repair the sagging walls of despair.
To rebuild it with the bricks of promises, faith and hard work.

♥ Mantra

I will rebuild my sagging wall of despair, brick-by-brick, each brick, a new story of promise, of health, of love, of joy, of family.
I will rebuild my wall with the new story filled with all the most wonderful things God has planned for me, waiting for me to claim with faith and diligent work.

EVEN DARKNESS HAS ITS WONDERS

I have learned that everything has its wonders
Even darkness. And silence.
Even betrayal.

All that the soul has been searching, has an uncanny way of showing up in these times.
The desert presents a rare, captivating landscape.
Even in dry desert grounds, flowers bloom.
The eyes begin to see beauty it has not seen or sensed before.

These times of darkness comes to cleanse the stains, the rust.
With stainless thoughts. Blameless words.
To be showered with an inner redeemed glow no darkness can steal.

If you're still standing, then you are meant to stand on higher grounds.
If your eyes still have sight, then your eyes are meant to behold brighter visions.

To stand in the raw glare of new sensations,
new delights,
new gifts,
new mercies that await,
This is our inheritance.

♥ Mantra

In the dry desert season of my life, I will begin to cultivate my heart so that desert flowers can bloom.

I have come to learn that there are lessons that can only be learned in the hard and dry season of my life.

I have come to learn that inner strength and resilience is forged in fiery flames.

So let me focus on the lessons I need to learn and be equipped with instead of focusing on the trail.

IF THE TRUTH SETS US FREE, UNTRUE WAYS ENSLAVE US

If the Truth sets you free
Then ways that are not true, to them, you and I become enslaved.

I started my career as a journalist, using my gift.
Then the headhunter of a software company approached me and offered me three times my salary to work for them,
As the team lead over all their technical writers.
Based on the money, I took the new position.
And soon I was stuck in the grind of corporate America.

Every now and then my restless soul would remind me that this was not my place.
The inner call, that awakens the soul seemed to be at a distance,
Like tiny shining commas squirming on a forgotten field.

But when the corporate air began to choke,
I did reach into the bowels of my being, feebly holding on to courage, to follow the breadcrumbs to my heart.
Now, no one can take away the inner fire.
This inner blaze of glory I have come to live in.
Let your truths set you free.

♥ Mantra

I will examine the paths I have chosen to take in life based not on my truths, but based on compromise. The compromise of comfort, of money, of ease, of security, that has led me to become dissatisfied.

I will make the courageous decision to choose my path in life, based on the truth that sets my soul free and not give in to the choice of compromise.

THE POWER TO REPROGRAM OUR MINDS

It made for trending tech news when the world's best player of what might be humankind's most complicated board game, the Chinese Go, was defeated on May 22, 2017 by Google's computer program, AlphaGo.

Uber is actively testing cars without drivers on the road. I was speaking to one of the team leaders of this revolutionary project, "the 360-degree laser beams on the cars means there will be no blind spots, no night vision loss, no tired drivers or drivers who text and drive, that threaten safety."

This level of human ingenuity is fascinating.

If we have been empowered to create machines of such unbelievable intelligence, how much more power has been poured onto the palm of our hands, transferred into our lifeblood, blasted into our brain cells,

To create and recreate the raw essence of who we are?

♥ Mantra

I have not been cognizant of the power that has been offered to me with this gift called life. I have often played victim and blamed my fate, when in fact I have the power to alter the course of my life, in the direction of my deepest desires.

I will take back my power and re-engineer my life in all the areas that need a reboot.

THE MIRACLE OF MOVEMENTS

As I was getting ready this morning, toothbrush in hand, raising my right arm,

It occurred to me what a miracle that simple task was.

How many hundreds of nerves and cells are functioning optimally within my body to perform this simple task?

There are thousands in hospitals whose nervous system has been damaged and can't perform this basic task.

There are thousands whose hearts failed and life left them during the night hours.

You woke up with eyes that can see,

A heart that is beating,

Feet that brought you to work.

The countless miracles that you and I are living today!

♥ Mantra

I am so thankful for health – for all the organs in my body that are functioning perfectly without me having to do any work.

My perfect body temperature.

My hands that deftly perform complex tasks so faithfully every day.

My feet, that occupy such little space yet carry my 100+ pounds, year after year.

How can I not be grateful, ever grateful?

LOVE THAT NEVER GROWS DULL AND NEVER WANES

Like sunlight that never grows dull or dim...
Like rain and snow that never runs out...
Like the moon that faithfully lights up the dark sky,
Each night a different version.
There is a Love that pursues us...

It never runs dry.
It never fades.
It never wanes.
It longs to restore every beaten and broken path within us.
It delights to shower us with new blessings.

It longs to walk with us, on the alleys of all our hopes and dreams...
The side streets down which we walk at night.
The wooded areas and the swamps.

It longs to be a part of the thoughts and feelings reserved for innermost communion.
The fires that burn on different altars of our lives.
It longs to walk Together by the edges still untold...
It is eager to fuse all our innermost parts to faith and the fire it sparks.

♥ Mantra

Today, I want to get out of my small mind and invite the Love that has been pursuing me all my life. I want to share my deepest desires and all my innermost thoughts and feelings with this Love that longs to be intimate with me.

HOPE HAS NO BOUNDARIES

Hope is a force engineered within our inner chambers,
Often stirred to its furthest limits in the deepest, darkest pit.
It sleeps no moment on an old past.
It becomes the overarching cloud of promise constantly hovering over us.
It follows us everywhere we go, in every season.

It is the shining, sticky substance that leaves a glimmer on everything it touches,
Stamps its sterling strength in every handshake and smile.

Faith. Hope. And Love.
The great attributes that we have all been built with.
Hope is the triumph of the heart.

♥ Mantra

I will embrace the fullness of hope into my life today, especially in all the areas of my life where I have given up hope.
I will allow hope to sit with me in all the places where I feel defeated.
I will let the outcome from hope become my tunnel vision reality.
I will achieve my goal by holding on to hope.

THE PRICE OF LIBERTY

Eternal vigilance is the price of liberty.
Liberty to use the blank canvas of our life and make with it what we will.

True liberty calls for true vigilance.
Vigilance over our thought life.
Vigilance over the food we eat.
Vigilance of the path our feet find steady ground. Vigilance over why we believe what we believe.

Vigilance to discover the secret stories hidden within the dust particles of our soul, Imprinted into the marrow of our bones.

Eternal vigilance over the colors of our life.
Eternal vigilance over how far the brush and sketch can extend its reach.
Liberty comes with a high price.

♥ Mantra

I will not take the gift of liberty lightly. I realize the cost that comes with freedom. I will treasure this liberty I have been gifted and use it with vigilance. I will use the blank canvas of life gifted to me and paint it with brush strokes that go a little further every day. I will be vigilant with my liberty to use it to create the life I desire.

WHEN LOVE BECOMES OUR WEAPON

When Love becomes the unchanging voice over all our trials,
Even as the brain belches up a double dose of pessimism...
When our desire to hold love as the banner over those who
inflicted us pain, becomes our resolute commitment.

When love becomes our daily obsession,
To be kind to all, to be patient, to overlook a wrong.
Our every step is protected.
Our days carefully orchestrated.
Every detail masterfully designed.

Above all, it blesses our inner world with dancing sunbeams in the
day.
And moonbeams at night.
Repels the tentacles of anger, bitterness and depression,
From finding a nesting place within us.
Love will never lose its Power.

♥ Mantra

I will choose to make Love my great obsession. When I face
thoughts that contradict loving thoughts towards others or toward
myself, I will actively work to replace it with thoughts of love
toward that person or myself.
Because thinking unloving thoughts only makes me small and
renders a sense of dis-ease within me.

I will consciously cultivate the presence of love within me at all hours of the day.

Then my life will be blessed with unending streams of joy.

THERE COMES A TIME

There comes a time when you are called to step out of the bleachers
And be a player on the field.
To embrace the visionary tics that shiver in the chest.

To dance with the sounds of forgotten music once inside you, now
drifting into the distance.
To court it again, to wrap its magic around your heart and offer the
world the unique notes that only you can sing.

When a young Ralph Lauren designed his wide ties contrary to the
prevailing fashion trend,
Asked to change it – he stood firm in faith that what he created
from his heart would prevail.

The memory of sitting in his office on Madison Ave, in Manhattan,
is still resplendent.
It lives inside me, an encounter that changed me.
I suppose structures and services birthed from the heart do that to
you.

How beautiful will this earth become if each of us rise up to the
visionary tics in our hearts.
We will all partake of each other's goods and services birthed from
true purpose and passion.

The earth will then breathe with a new strength,
As goods and services will be birthed from all our dreams and
visions.
We, just have to dare to step out of the sidelines of safety.

Whether or not we're consciously following our Destiny
Our unique destiny is always following us.

♥ Mantra

I will take some time out today: a walk, a drive, a couch - to meditate, and to reflect. And I will dance with the sounds of the forgotten music that my soul once danced with. I will begin to awaken the dreams that I let drift away.
I will remember my forgotten music.

CREATED TO BE LIVING FLAMES

We were created to be living flames.

Each of us, with our unique flame, lighting up the landscapes of this dark earth.

We are all drawn to the those whose flames are burning bright.

The zeal of the innovator who wants to connect the world through technology.

The passion of the businessman who can create money out of thin air.

The love of the mother or mentor whose life is bright and seeks to give wings to the fledgling.

The dream of the painter who paints pictures to draw us into their place of darkness, wonder or glory.

Sometimes, the flame waits to be summoned again.

Often, it is found in the violent fires.

It is found when beset with poverty and abandoned, a little Oprah Winfrey watched her grandmother hanging clothes on a clothesline, but dreamed of a bright life beyond, where only her little mind could travel.

It is found when raped as a seven-year-old Maya Angelou stopped speaking, remained mute for almost six years,

But became a prolific reader, diving into literature.

Raped and mute, yet blossoming in the pit of dismay, to a world of literature and great writers, until one day, she would become one.

To be bright, living flames, lighting up the world, with our own unique fire and its unique flame.

♥ Mantra

I recognize yet again, that it is often in the darkest season of my life that I am being forged with indomitable strength.

I want to live my life as a bright living flame, offering my unique fire and light to the world.

I will remember that it is in the fiercest of fires that my incorruptible life flame is often found.

THE HIGH FROM LIFE WE ALL SEEK

We are all seeking a high from life, and rightly so.

It's hardwired into our beings.

Liquor stores and drugs that promise a 'high' are trillion dollar industries.

We are constantly offered new types of thrills: porn, waterparks, movies, skydiving – the list is endless and the choices for thrilling experiences keep growing.

There is another path to the 'high' we are all after.

It was carved out for us, thousands of years ago.

It is a path that never becomes dated, it has stood the test of time, century after century.

This path is not decked out or alluring to the eye, it is plain and lowly.

Soft sounds of freedom twinkle in the song of the winds,

The great initiative is ours to take.

As you take a step, you discover fairies and angels, dancing in ever-flowing waters,

Iron shoes weighed with worry become light, and you find yourself waltzing freely.

Silver and gold paths beam right inside of you with inner peace, its glittering rays never quite leaving you, even in the piercing chills of an alpine winter.

In the starless midnight, the sweetest voice whispers, soothes memory and reality.

The food for all our hopes is found here.

The thrill for all our adventures abounds in this place.

Everything we hold dear, is cradled here.

It cherishes our every hope and makes it bloom like a tender flower.

♥ Mantra

I feel humbled and honored that I am the one who needs to take the initiative to invite this radical, joy-filled journey of life as mine

The invitation to walk hand-in-hand with Everlasting Love and the magical world this love connection offers us entry into.

It transforms every damaged and dull path to a new shining pathway, lit with the brightest colors and ringing with the happiest songs.

TO FIGHT THE GOOD FIGHT

To fight the good fight with the weapons of goodness,
It's what we are called to do.

To fight the fears. To fight the lie that you are not significant.
To fight the battle of self-hatred.
To fight the life sucking virus of small beliefs.
To fight to preserve our life motor: our heart, soft and alive even in the face of abuse and heartbreak.

To fight the battle of jealousy that insidiously creeps into our minds,
To fight the battle of living on the complacent grounds built by the status quo.

To fight. And to keep fighting.
Because there is a story written in the stars.
Woven into our hearts.
The whisper held in the embrace of the Thunder.

Because nothing will ever quite fully satisfy,
Until we're living and breathing in our story that was written in the stars.

♥ Mantra

I will fight the good fight. The fight for things that keep me alive within, which is where it ultimately and truly matters.

I will fight to become all that I was meant to become.

I will resist being stuck in the shallow pools of compromise that brings lethargy and lack.

I will keep fighting to arise to become the greatest and the highest version of me that I dare to envision.

THE CHAOTIC DRUMBEATS OF OUR TIMES

In the midst of the chaotic drumbeats reverberating through our land,

Suicide and depression have reached epic proportions.

In the midst of the braided band that binds us,

We are called to remember that we were created to function as multi-dimensional beings.

We were created to enjoy food for our body, but also the food from heaven to satisfy our deepest hunger.

We were created to always be loved,

Anything less dispossess us from our inner serene state.

We were created to know that we can always be held in Everlasting Arms.

We were created to live in the continual joy that wells up from communing daily with Everlasting Love.

Nothing less can truly fulfill our longings:

Our highest joys,

Our deepest longings...

Our desire for unending pleasures.

Our secret searching for something more than we cannot quite place a finger on.

♥ Mantra

Spirit lead me to this sacred place where all my longings can be fulfilled. I have looked to people and places to satisfy me, but it only left me disappointed.

Everlasting arms of unconditional love is what I was created for, here all my deepest longings burn alive, and find their home.

TRUTH SEEKS TO TRANSFORM OUR LIVES

All that we will ever truly know in the deep places,
Must pass through the gateway of our experience.
Till it leaves us bathed in delightful transmutation –
A new pair of eyes that will never grow dull.

But our deep truths are often only found by wading through dark waters.
It is gained at a great cost.

When truth seeks us, it is often nestled as a bright kernel shrouded in phantoms of fear.
Because we are prone to back out and take the easy way out, it comes back to revisit.
Old familiar events seem to beat upon our lives again.
Until we have learned to lean in and learn the lessons.

Then the day arrives when we wear the new truth like a necklace of diamonds,
Around the neck of our memory.
Like a gold covenant ring on the finger of recollection.
And we finally realize that the tests came for a great purpose.
To liberate us. Forever. From the clutches of fear.

♥ Mantra

Today I will allow new truth and it's healing power to find me. I will not shun, or run away, when truth comes disguised inside a trial, when truth comes to bless my life through a difficult circumstance.

God give me the strength to accept the trial and search for the hidden lesson I need to learn, even through the trial, that will challenge me to grow.

FAITH THE PERMANENT SECURITY OF THE HEART

Faith is the gray dawn that precedes the brightest sunrise.
Faith is the fire that moves our sinking feet forward.

Faith is the fuel that has more force than every visible opposing reality.
Faith is the raging, radiant fever that never seems to let up.

Faith is the permanent security of the heart.
Faith is the friend of the feeble.

♥ Mantra

I will walk by faith today. I will make faith the ruling power of my life. Faith will carry me all the days of my life even on rough violent seas.
Faith will become my calming anchor.

SHADOWS OF THE PAST

Shadows of the past are often some of the biggest stumbling blocks to the greater life being offered to us.

So few strive to rip the tattered garments of the past.

These dismal shadows, they show up, catching us unaware, in the middle minutes.

Along the tracks of the everyday life.

The minutes we want to climb out of, or even remain in.

The choice, really, is up to us.

Bruce H. Lipton, PhD, a stem cell biologist and an international leader in bridging science and spirit, states 95% of our lives are programmed by others, that become habit patterns we live out.

He suggests taking powerful words, like what Jesus boldly claims – 'Behold I made all things new' and combine it with the Buddhist art of meditation of being present, consciously feeding our thoughts to rewrite the old records with new bright records.

I was trying to re-write my own past records with a new one, inspired by a song I listened to during my morning workout session today.

> *"There's no shadow You won't light up*
> *Mountain You won't climb up coming after me.*
> *There's no wall You won't kick down*
> *Lie You won't tear down, coming after me."*

Reckless Love – Cory Asbury

♥ Mantra

Today, I will write a new story over the story with dark shadows that frequently comes to disrupt my peace, and to make me feel small.

I now write and speak a new story over this story. With the power of my thoughts and imagination, I write a new story over this persisting dark shadow.

(Spend some time in meditation to imagine and re-write the new story. Replace the negative story with positive images from the new story)

The reflections of my new vision are so bright now that it blinds the negative thoughts with the brightness of the new images.

HEART BELIEF VS MIND BELIEF

Heart-belief is quite different from mind-belief.

Heart-belief is like an invisible web of sparkling diamonds formed in the crucible of life's fire,

Now glittering over every conscious and subconscious thought.

Mind-belief is a more superficial knowing, it enters in the form of a new thought.

It sits in the prefrontal cortex of the brain as a foreign body.

It is often deposited in a classroom, a business meeting, a conference, a study – as new knowledge.

Heart-beliefs run deeper than deep.

Higher than high.

It courses through our whole being.

Where it begins and where it ends, we cannot tell; just that its power prevails over every obstacle, and every fire.

Its miraculous, transformative power pulses through all the hidden veins.

When we can take our mind-belief and place it in the region of heart-belief,

Our inner atmosphere begins to delightfully transform.

That we would yield our lives from mind-beliefs to radiant heart-beliefs, about our own self.

As we begin the new workout, the diet, the financial goal, the new personal goal; operating from heart-beliefs, by remembering who we truly are!

\#Schoolofgratitute \#mindmastery \#thepowerofbelief

♥ Mantra

I will actively engage my thoughts to create the most powerful truth I want to manifest in my life. I will stay in this new truth till my mind-belief becomes heart-belief.

I will stay focused, and find great joy in allowing my heart-beliefs to become my daily reality.

LIFE, MEANT TO BE A GRAND CELEBRATION

I believe that Life was meant to be a grand celebration.

Of being held in wild, exuberant, unconditional love –

But we believe we're not good enough.

A celebration of our souls,

But we've learned to squelch its power because it was often not heart.

A celebration of our minds,

But we've tamed it to succumb to societal norms.

A celebration of our bodies – but we're mostly dissatisfied by it.

A celebration of sex, but we feel guilty if we enjoy it too much.

A celebration of food - but it's often ridden by fear.

A celebration of friendships – but it gets crowded by jealousy and comparison.

A celebration of wealth – but we hoard it or think it's wrong to have too much.

These, in its purest forms were meant to be life's great gifts to us.

Sadly, we have allowed our lives to be courted for years with all its counterfeits.

But we can all return to its purest, richest live-giving forms.

We just have to make the choice and then set out to search for these great, vigorous high roads.

Hardships and heartaches; the obstacles we will have to overcome along the way.

♥ Mantra

I will change my belief that life is hard, to a new belief that life is meant to be beautiful and easy.

Life is meant to be celebrated.

I will celebrate all the beauty of nature surrounding me.

I will learn to start celebrating who I am.

I will celebrate my authentic self.

I will celebrate my body.

I will celebrate my mind.

I will celebrate my heart.

I will celebrate my dreams.

I will celebrate the real Me.

Made in the USA
San Bernardino, CA
27 March 2019